Witness History Series

THE COLD WAR

Derek Heater

Wayland

Titles in this series

The Arab-Israeli Conflict
China since 1945
The Cold War
The Origins of the First World War
The Russian Revolution
South Africa since 1948
The Third Reich
The United Nations

Cover illustration: Guarding the Berlin wall.

First published in 1989 by
Wayland (Publishers) Ltd
61 Western Road, Hove
East Sussex BN3 1JD, England

© Copyright 1989 Wayland (Publishers) Ltd

Editor: Catherine Ellis
Designer: Ross George
Consultant: Dr Michael Dunne, lecturer in American studies at
the University of Sussex

British Library Cataloguing in Publication Data
Heater, Derek, 1931–
  The cold war. – (Witness history)
  1. Western bloc countries. Foreign
  relations with communist countries. 2.
  Communist countries. Foreign relations with
  Western bloc countries.
  I. Title. II. Series
  327′.09171′3

ISBN 1-85210-656-5

Typeset by Kalligraphics Limited, Horley, Surrey
Printed and bound by Sagdos, S.p.A., Milan

327.09.

Contents

1

GROWTH OF SUSPICION
East–West relations 1917–45

. . . *under Truman and his equally obstinate and aggressive Secretary of State, that political half wit Mr Acheson, American foreign policy was calculated to provoke and bully us from a position of strength.*[1]

Let us pray for those who live in that totalitarian darkness, pray they will discover the joy of knowing God. But, until they do . . . they are the focus of evil in the modern world.[2]

THE FIRST QUOTATION is from the Soviet leader, Nikita Khrushchev, describing his view of US policy towards his country in the years immediately after the Second World War. The second is from a speech by the US President, Ronald Reagan in 1983, explaining his view of the Soviet Union. These extracts are typical of the hatred, fear and suspicion with which these two countries have faced each other for so many years. Luckily for the whole world, however, they have hurled only insults at each

Soldiers and civilians parading through the streets of Petrograd (now Leningrad) in 1917, expressing comradeship in support of the Bolshevik revolution.

other, not missiles. The rivalry and conflict between them is known as the Cold War, because in all their power struggles in flashpoints around the world, and in the nuclear arms race, they have never actually come to direct military confrontation, never met in the 'heat' of battle.

Although the freeze in international relations really set in after the Second World War, it is possible to trace its origins from the time when the Bolshevik communists took control of Russia in 1917 and civil war broke out. Several countries, including the USA, Britain and France, sent troops to fight with the counter-revolutionary 'White Armies' against the communists. These and other governments of the Western countries did not like communism and their views were reinforced by the horrors of Stalin's purges. Stalin was Soviet dictator for about thirty years and in the 1930s he had millions of his opponents either killed or imprisoned.

The Allied leaders, Churchill, Roosevelt and Stalin, are seen here with their advisers at Yalta in 1945.

After 1941 the USA, Britain and the USSR were allies in the struggle against Nazi Germany. But relations, especially between Stalin and the British Prime Minister, Churchill, were never very easy.

Towards the end of the war the Allied leaders began to have meetings to arrange what should happen in Europe after the defeat of Germany. The most important was the Yalta Conference. At this Russian seaside resort Stalin, Churchill and Roosevelt agreed that the frontiers of Poland should be changed, that Germany should be divided into zones of occupation, and that the Russians should be able to make sure that the countries of Eastern Europe would be friendly towards them. All these decisions were to cause future trouble between the Soviet Union and the West.

Communism v. capitalism

The political and ideological differences between the Soviet Union and the West are so fundamental that over the years it has been practically impossible for them to find any friendly common ground or to do anything which did not make the other side feel threatened.

One side in this rivalry, led by the Soviet Union, is communist. Communism is the set of beliefs developed mainly by the German writer Karl Marx in the nineteenth century. He argued that divisions between social classes have always been important in history. He believed that the clash of interests between the workers (proletariat) and the capitalist middle-class businessmen (bourgeoisie) would, sooner or later, burst out into revolution and that such a revolution would eventually spread over the whole world until all class differences were destroyed. A new, just kind of life would then come about with wealth shared out fairly.

With the Bolshevik Revolution Russia became the first country to plan to become communist. The revolution did not, however, spread throughout the world as Marx had predicted. The Bolshevik leader, Lenin, explained this by pointing out that the workers in countries like the USA and Britain were benefiting from an artificially high standard of living. This was made possible

Stalin forced the richer, land-owning Soviet peasants (the kulaks) to give up their land. This photograph, taken in 1930, shows kulaks leaving their village to work in factories.

▲ Ever since Stalin's attack on the kulaks, agriculture and the production of food have been serious problems in the USSR. This photograph, taken in 1983, shows a queue for sausage, the only meat available.

▼ One way in which the industry of capitalist countries was used from the 1920s was to produce motor cars. This photograph shows an English Austin in 1922.

because of the cheap food produced by the wretchedly poor people of foreign lands controlled by the capitalist countries, and Lenin thought that these people abroad should rebel against 'imperial control'.

In contrast, the governments and people of most Western countries, such as the USA and Britain, believe in political freedom and capitalism. Some people, especially in the USA, have passionately argued that the kind of equality that communism stands for can only be achieved, if at all, by making life drab and brutally suppressing any criticism of the system. They believe that communist control and planning is inefficient, that manufacturers and businessmen will be more efficient if they know they can enjoy the profits from their work, and that the wealthier a whole country becomes in this way the more likely it will be that most people will benefit.

Both sides are determined that their system must be made to prevail – either by open war, or by propaganda, tricks and competition, falling short of actual fighting.

View from the USA

From 1917 to 1945 there were only two communist countries in the world – the USSR and (from 1924) Mongolia. By examining the map you can see how quickly other countries became communist in the 1940s. In 1939–40 the Soviet Union seized a long strip of land from Finland to the Black Sea. After the Second World War Russian influence ensured that communist governments came to power in much of Eastern Europe, and over these countries led to their being called 'satellites'. Large numbers of Soviet troops remained in Eastern Europe. In the late 1940s the communist parties were very strong in Greece, France and Italy, and for a while it looked as though they might take control. In Asia, communist governments had already come to power in China and North Korea, and strong communist forces

fought to gain control in the Philippines, Malaya, Indonesia and Indo-China.

To many politicians in Washington it appeared as though their opposite numbers in Moscow were master-minding a great expansion of communism. In 1946 the American ambassador in Moscow, George Kennan, sent the famous 'long telegram' to Washington. He warned that the Russians could not be trusted. The next year he published an article in which he stated:

It is clear that the main element of any United States policy towards the Soviet Union must be that of a long term, patient but firm and vigilant containment of Russian expansive tendencies.[3]

The spread of communist influence.

GERMANY

AUSTRIA
CZECHO
SLOVAKIA
POLAND
HUNGARY
YUGOSLAVIA
ROMANIA
ALBANIA
BULGARIA
GREECE

GREECE
(1947)

BERLIN (1949)
CZECHOSLOVAKIA (1948)

U S S R

INDO-CHINA
(1946)

MALAYSIA
(1948)

PHILIPPINES
(1949)

KOREA
(1950)

Key to inset:
— Iron Curtain as defined by Churchill
Countries occupied by Russian armies or with communist governments after 1945
Territory gained by USSR since 1939
Russian occupation zones

Key to map:
Soviet annexations
USSR allies
Yugoslavia
★ Communist aggression

▲ Some people were brave enough to protest against the anti-communist fear in the USA in the 1950s. This shows a group of film personalities (including such big names as Humphrey Bogart, Lauren Bacall, Danny Kaye) after a protest meeting.

▶ Julius and Ethel Rosenberg were executed in 1951 for supplying the USSR with atomic bomb secrets.

The US President, Truman, was convinced. 'Containment' became US policy. Every effort was to be made to stop Russia helping communists to gain control in any other countries.

In the 1950s US determination to stop the spread of communism became even more intense. John Foster Dulles, who was Secretary of State (foreign minister) from 1953 to 1959, spoke of 'rolling back' communism from Eastern Europe and 'going to the brink' of nuclear war to force the Russians to retreat. The American Senator Joseph McCarthy started a terrifying 'witch-hunt', and made wild accusations that treacherous communists were in important positions in the United States and must be hunted down and 'weeded out'.

View from the Soviet Union

When Stalin took over control of the Soviet Union in the 1920s he was very conscious that it was a backward country compared with highly industrialized states like the USA, Germany and Britain, but it was these Western countries who were the particular enemies of communism. Stalin therefore set about developing factories at an amazing speed to make Russia an up-to-date military power. In 1931 he defended this policy, saying: 'We are fifty or a hundred years behind the advanced countries. We must make

good this distance in ten years. Either we do it, or they will crush us.'[4]

In 1941, ten years after Stalin made this speech, Hitler launched an invasion of the USSR. Four years later the war was at an end, but at what cost to the Russians! It is

Builders are shown here constructing a factory for the making of tractors. This was part of one of Stalin's Five Year Plans to rapidly develop Soviet industry and agriculture.

The ruins of Riga, capital of Latvia in the USSR, devastated during the Second World War.

estimated that 20 million people lost their lives, and untold millions, probably more than those killed, were wounded. Cities, towns and villages had been pounded into ruins and vast areas of farmland and quantities of livestock were destroyed. Considering such a scale of loss it is little wonder that Stalin wanted there to be friendly, communist governments in Eastern Europe to act as a barrier against any future attack from the West.

Stalin believed that the USSR was in peril from capitalist encirclement. From 1949 to 1955 the USA helped to organize its allies into three military groupings: the North Atlantic Treaty Organization (NATO) in Western Europe and North America, the Baghdad Pact in the Middle East, and the South East Asia Treaty Organization (SEATO) in the Far East. In addition to these alliances, the USA had military, air force

and naval bases in other countries such as Japan and powerful fleets patrolling the oceans. Was Stalin's fear justified in the context of the West's military situation?

At that time the USA could probably have attacked the Soviet Union fairly effectively, whereas the Russians were not in such a strong position. In 1945 the USA had the only atom bombs then in existence, and the USSR had none until 1949. By 1952 the USA had developed the far more powerful hydrogen or thermo-nuclear bomb, and furthermore they had efficient long-range bombers (Superfortresses), some of which were based in Britain. The Russians, on the other hand, were slow to build a bomber fleet. They felt understandably vulnerable.

2
EUROPE DIVIDED
The Iron Curtain

IMMEDIATELY AFTER the Second World War, for all the differences and suspicions between East and West, many politicians hoped for friendly relations with Russia. It soon became evident, however, that this would not be so, and the Cold War took a hold in Europe. The Russians were determined to keep control over Eastern Europe, and they managed this in three ways. Firstly, they intervened to ensure that the communist parties gained control of the East European governments. Secondly, large numbers of the Russian troops who had arrived in Eastern Europe for the purpose of defeating the Germans stayed on to help these new communist governments to remain in power. Finally, to stop outside interference, very few visitors were allowed from Western countries.

In March 1946 Winston Churchill gloomily surveyed the scene in a speech he delivered in the USA: 'From Stettin in the Baltic,' he said, 'to Trieste in the Adriatic, an iron curtain has descended across the continent'.[5] The phrase conjured up a vivid picture and the states of Eastern Europe are still sometimes known as 'iron curtain countries'.

During the next two years the Soviet Union tightened its grip on the region. In 1947 it set up the Communist Information Bureau (Cominform) to control the communist parties of Eastern Europe, (and also Italy and France). At the end of the war, of all the countries of Eastern Europe, the communists were least popular in Czechoslovakia, but by 1948 they had seized power there also.

The biggest blow to Western politicians, however, was the communist control of Poland. The Second World War had started because Britain and France had objected to Hitler's attack on Poland. To end the war with another foreign rule in Poland, and the Polish people still unable to choose their own government freely, was bitterly ironic. Study the map on page 8. Why do you think Poland was of such vital importance to the Russians?

Look at the map opposite. How did the Allies deal with Germany and with its old capital of Berlin in 1945? Which portion did Russia control? These arrangements were intended to be temporary, but the Russians and the Western occupying powers could not agree on a permanent solution.

Most of the US and British forces were demobilized after the war and left Europe. Many Soviet soldiers, on the other hand, remained.

Winston Churchill, British prime minister during the Second World War, coined the term 'Iron Curtain' while on a visit to the USA.

▲ After the Second World War the USA and Britain were quick to send most of their armed forces back to civilian life. This photograph shows RAF men being 'demobbed'.

▶ At the end of the war the division of Germany into four sectors left Berlin marooned. The air corridors are the routes into Berlin taken by Western planes during the Berlin airlift (see page 16).

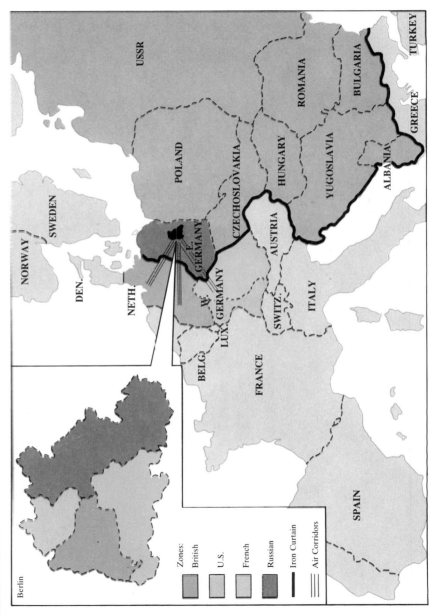

NORWAY

SWEDEN

USSR

DEN.

NETH.

E. GERMANY

POLAND

W. GERMANY

CZECHOSLOVAKIA

LUX.

BELG.

AUSTRIA

HUNGARY

ROMANIA

FRANCE

SWITZ.

ITALY

YUGOSLAVIA

BULGARIA

ALBANIA

GREECE

TURKEY

SPAIN

Berlin

Zones:
British
U.S.
French
Russian
Iron Curtain
Air Corridors

US support for Europe

There was a slim chance immediately after the war that tension might be relaxed between the East and West. But US policies outlined in two crucial speeches in 1947 made this impossible. What was it about these speeches that so hardened the division of Europe?

The first was a speech by US President Truman to Congress. He was worried by the strength of the communists fighting a civil war in Greece, and by Russian attempts to force Turkey to allow Soviet warships through the Straits of the Bosphorus and Dardanelles. He wanted Congress to approve the spending of money to help countries like these 'threatened by communism'. In his speech he painted a stark picture and proposed the solution known as the Truman Doctrine:

Was Stalin planning to extend communist control to Greece and therefore the Mediterranean, as Truman feared? The following extract is from a conversation the following February in which Stalin stated that the Greek guerilla fighters:

This Italian family greatly improved its farm output, helped by money supplied through Marshall Aid.

. . . have no prospect of success at all. What, do you think that Great Britain and the United States . . . will permit you to break their line of communication in the Mediterranean? Nonsense. And we have no navy. The uprising in Greece must be stopped, and as quickly as possible. [7]

What does this suggest about Stalin's intentions and confidence?

Truman was no doubt influenced by Kennan's ideas on 'containment', and also by the weak condition of the West European economies. In 1947 Britain was almost bankrupted by five years of all-out war and on the European continent factories and communications systems lay in ruins from land fighting and aerial bombardment. These countries needed help.

Three months after President Truman's speech his Secretary of State, George Marshall, proposed that the USA should help the stricken countries. The offer was open to all European states, East as well as West. Truman called it 'one of America's greatest contributions to the peace of the world'. [8] Stalin thought otherwise. He had no intention of allowing capitalists to interfere in Eastern Europe. The Organization for European Economic Co-operation (OEEC) was set up to administer this European Recovery Programme, or Marshall Aid as it was called. The graph below shows how the funds were allocated. How does this reveal a divided Europe? Do you think that Truman and Marshall were in any way responsible for furthering the Cold War, or did Truman contribute to the 'peace of the world'?

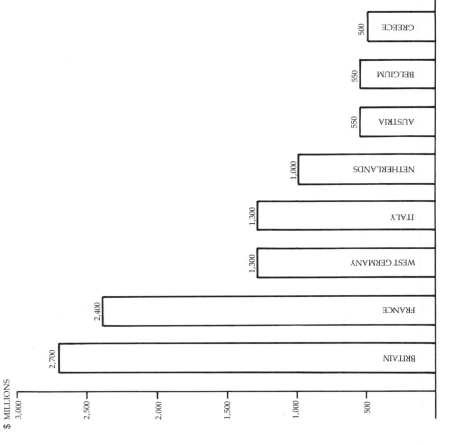

Graph showing the countries that received Marshall Aid 1948-51.

The problem of Berlin

At the end of the Second World War one of the biggest problems facing the Allies was deciding upon the future of Germany. The Western occupying powers – Britain, the USA and France – wanted Germany to be reunited so that its economy could recover, and as a bulwark against the USSR. The Russians, however, wanted to keep it divided because twice in fifty years German armies had penetrated deep into their country, causing huge casualties and damage. By the summer of 1948, with no agreement in sight, the Western powers introduced a new currency in their zones. The Russians suspected plans to unify these zones and took action.

Look at the position of Berlin on the map on page 13. What difficulties were there likely to be in keeping West Berlin supplied with food, fuel and other necessities? In June 1948 the Russians blocked the railway and road routes into Berlin which passed through Soviet-controlled land. The Western governments pondered on how to act. Should they surrender Berlin? Should they force supplies through with escorts of tanks? What would be the likely effect have been on the Cold War of each of these actions?

In the end a third option was tried and was remarkably successful. For eleven months the two million inhabitants of West Berlin were supplied from the air. Transport aircraft made 277,728 flights with loads totalling 2,380,794 tonnes. The Berlin airlift, as it was known, was an extraordinary achievement. The Russians had to admit defeat and reopened the land routes in May 1949.

Later in 1949, within months of the blockade, West and East Germany became separate countries. Berlin, however, remained a source of tension. The communists objected to the presence of Western troops and officials in the heart of East Germany, and they were embarrassed that so many East Germans fled to the West – over three million

During the Berlin airlift planes carrying essential supplies were landing every three minutes. Here a huge US plane is being unloaded of its cargo of twenty tonnes of flour.

▼ In recent years parts of the Berlin Wall on the Western side have been decorated and daubed with graffiti and slogans.

▼ A check-point at Friedrichstrasse between the US and Soviet zones in Berlin. This photograph was taken in October 1961. Notice the tanks guarding each side.

left between 1945 and 1961 – but the West would not give up its position. The US President, Kennedy, explained the reason in a broadcast in 1961:

[Berlin] is more than a showcase of liberty, a symbol, an island of freedom in a Communist sea. It is even more than a link with the free world, a beacon of hope behind the Iron Curtain, an escape hatch for refugees. . . above all it has become, as never before, a great testing place of Western courage and will.[9]

Three weeks later the East Germans built a wall to stop their people escaping. This was a formidable barrier, illuminated by search-lights at night and guarded by armed soldiers, who shot anyone who tried to get through. Although they argued the Berlin Wall was to keep Western spies out, it in fact became a powerful symbol of communist imprisonment. Were the Western governments right to remain so firm over the question of Berlin?

NATO and the Warsaw Pact

The communist overthrow of the democratic government in Czechoslovakia in 1948 and events in Berlin shocked Western leaders. Was there a real danger at this stage, however, of a Soviet invasion of Western Europe? Would you alter your opinion in the light of the following comments by British, American and Canadian historians respectively about the European military situation in 1948?

The Soviets had 140 divisions, 25 of them in Central Europe, whereas the Americans had only 2½ divisions in Germany. [10]

By early 1948, the Red Army (including apparently the air force) would be down to 2,874,000 men . . . The Russian figure of early 1948 can be roughly compared to the ceilings for the American military for July 1, 1947 – 1,070,000 in the Army; 558,000 in the Navy; 108,000 in the Marines. The British armed services contained well over a million men. [11]

. . . future secretary of state John Foster Dulles testified before a congressional committee that he did 'not know of any responsible high official, military or civilian . . . who believes that the Soviet [Union] now plans conquest by open military aggression.' [12]

Each May Day, which is a public holiday in the Soviet Union, a great military display is held in Moscow. This parade of missiles took place in 1964 and illustrates Soviet might.

President Harry S. Truman formally signing the North Atlantic Treaty in July 1949.

In 1949, to improve the West's defences a new organization – the North Atlantic Treaty Organization (NATO) – was brought into existence. The British Foreign Secretary, Ernest Bevin, was particularly anxious that the USA should keep armed forces in Western Europe. On 4 April 1949 twelve states (ten European countries, USA and Canada) signed the North Atlantic Treaty, establishing a military alliance. This declared that:

> . . . an armed attack against one or more of them in Europe or North America shall be considered an attack against them all.[13]

The US General Eisenhower was appointed NATO's first Supreme Allied Commander in Europe, and the forces at his disposal were steadily increased. Other commanders were appointed for the Atlantic and English Channel fleets. The basic idea was to co-ordinate the armed forces of the countries in the North Atlantic area; for example, the forces stationed in Europe were commanded by Eisenhower from a central headquarters in Paris. Over the years more countries joined NATO, including West Germany in 1955. France, however, while remaining a member of the alliance, began to remove its forces from the NATO central command in 1966. The European headquarters was then moved to Belgium.

The USSR was angry about the creation of NATO and especially the inclusion of West Germany. In 1955, a week after West Germany joined NATO, the USSR countered by establishing a similar organization, the Warsaw Pact. Both alliances still exist.

3

THE FAR & MIDDLE EAST
Conflict 1945–73

SIX MONTHS AFTER the signing of the North Atlantic Treaty, Mao Zedong proclaimed the establishment of the Communist Chinese People's Republic. A civil war had been raging in China between the communists and the Nationalist government of Jiang Jieshi for many years. When he was defeated he retreated with his government to the island of Taiwan. Jiang Jieshi's defeat was a great shock to America, his major ally. Not only had their ally been forced to retreat, but the new government of China was communist. Until the 1970s

the USA continued to support the Nationalist Government on Taiwan in the hope that it would regain power. The US Seventh Fleet patrolled the area, and the USA refused to allow the Chinese communists to take the Chinese seat in the United Nations. Meanwhile, the USA encouraged Jiang Jieshi in his threat to invade the mainland to re-establish the

Mao Zedong reading the proclamation which founded the Communist Chinese People's Republic, 1 October 1949.

Soviet-made military vehicles used by the Syrian army on the Golan Heights, the border area between Israel and Syria. Over the years both the USSR and the West have supplied military equipment to the Middle East.

Nationalist government there.

In the years after the Second World War, communist parties tried to gain power in several other Asian countries. After the war Korea was divided: the northern portion was occupied by Russia (where a communist government was established), and the southern portion by the USA. In 1950 the North Koreans invaded South Korea. Both China and the USA became involved in the struggle, the Chinese on the side of the communist North, the USA on the side of the South Koreans. The pattern of US intervention against communism in Asia was repeated in Vietnam in the bitterly fought conflict that began in the 1950s.

Although the USA worried about 'the spread of international communism', in fact the two major communist states, the USSR and China, were far from being allies. Mao thought the Soviet leader, Khrushchev, to be an upstart and mistaken in his policies. In 1960, the Russians who were helping to develop Chinese industry were ordered back to the Soviet Union. In 1969 fighting broke out on the border between the two countries.

The US concern about Russian influence also extended to the Middle East. The Suez Canal is a vital part of the sea route from Europe to the Gulf and the Far East, and the countries in the Gulf area are crucial sources of oil. Since 1945 the British and Americans have been nervous about any political instability in these areas or evidence of Russia interfering in the region, especially in Syria, Lebanon, Egypt and Iran. Over the years both the USSR and the West have sponsored and supported individual countries in the Middle East. How do you think this has affected the Cold War?

The Korean War

The North Korean army invaded South Korea on 25 June 1950. In less than six months they captured almost the whole country. This attack raises two important questions: did the Russians organize the invasion, and why were the North Koreans so successful?

Several US historians have argued that the war was part of a planned expansion of communism. A South Korean book claims:

The origin of the Korean War can be traced to Stalin's policy of aggressive imperialism. Such an interpretation is summarized in the brief statement by [the US professor] David J. Dallin that the Korean War was 'planned, prepared, and initiated by Stalin'.[14]

The Americans obviously supported South Korea, hoping to keep back the communists, and they succeeded in gaining the help of many other countries by presenting the problem to the United Nations, which blamed North Korea. The Russians, however, seem to have been taken by surprise. The USSR was not attending the UN at the time and therefore could not defend its ally. What does this suggest about whether the USSR planned the invasion or not?

One possible explanation for the speedy success of the North Korean army is that the US forces that had been in South Korea since 1945 had been withdrawn in 1949, and

A US tank using a flame-thrower to attack a Chinese position during the Korean War.

This photograph tries to emphasize the fact that the Korean War was a United Nations operation. Notice the UN flag. The soldiers are from Australia, the USA, South Korea and the Philippines. Korea was a rare instance of effective UN intervention.

the South Korean army was not yet properly trained and equipped to defend its country. South Korea did not expect such an unprovoked, full-scale invasion. But is there another possible reason? Ten years later a US journalist wrote that:

> . . . millions of South Koreans welcomed the prospect of unification, even on communist terms. They had suffered police brutality, intellectual repression and political purge. Few felt much incentive to fight for profiteers or to die for Syngman Rhee [head of the South Korean government].[15]

The Korean war was bitterly fought. The US General MacArthur was given command of all the troops fighting under the UN flag, and they pushed the North Koreans back to their frontier with China. Chinese troops then arrived to back the North Koreans and the UN forces retreated to roughly the North-South Korean border. Civilians as well as soldiers suffered – their homes were destroyed and many were killed. MacArthur wanted to invade China; maybe even to use atomic bombs, and President Truman dismissed him because of the horrible danger of the war spreading. The war eventually ended in a stalemate in 1953 with the old borders restored.

Indo-China

Violent as the Korean War was, the struggles in Indo-China were even more horrific. When the Second World War came to an end France's colonies in south-east Asia wanted independence. In Vietnam a guerrilla organization called the Vietminh, dedicated to ridding Vietnam of French rule, was started by the communist Ho Chi Minh. The Vietminh fought the French, and defeated them in a great battle at Dien Bien Phu. In 1954 Vietnam was divided and Ho Chi Minh became head of the communist government in North Vietnam.

The governments of Laos, Cambodia and especially South Vietnam were not very popular, so the communist parties had some support in the region. The USA was therefore understandably afraid that one by one the countries of south-east Asia would 'fall like dominoes' (as President Eisenhower

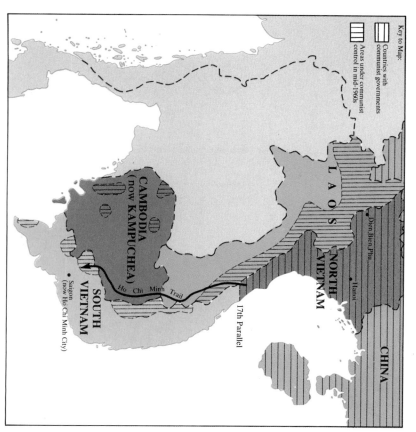

Key to Map:
- Countries with communist governments
- Areas under communist control in mid-1960s

CHINA

LAOS

NORTH VIETNAM

Dien Bien Phu

Hanoi

CAMBODIA (now KAMPUCHEA)

Ho Chi Minh Trail

17th Parallel

SOUTH VIETNAM

Saigon (now Ho Chi Minh City)

expressed it) to communism.

By 1960 the communist organization in South Vietnam, the National Liberation Front, known in the West as the Vietcong, were causing the government considerable trouble. Partly through intimidation they were taking over control of many villages. The US government decided to send 'advisers' to help the government of South Vietnam to fight the Vietcong, but not actually to fight themselves. Inevitably the US were soon drawn into the war, as were the North Vietnamese. US aircraft bombed North Vietnam, and dropped chemicals to strip foliage from trees to try to find the Vietcong camps. Horrific injury and destruction was caused by US fire-bombs made of napalm – a substance which sticks to buildings and flesh as it burns. The idea that such tactics would break the Vietcong

By the 1954 Geneva Accord Vietnam was temporarily partitioned at the 17th parallel, dividing the Vietminh in the north from the French and non-Vietminh in the south. Elections were to be held in 1956 for a government of a reunified Vietnam. Failure to hold them helped lead to civil war and chaos in the south.

One of the most famous photographs taken during the Vietnam War. It shows terrified children running down Highway One during an aerial napalm attack.

was misconceived; if anything they increased support for the Vietcong among the rural population. US involvement in the Vietnam War has been the subject of fierce controversy ever since.

Despite the great strength of the USA it could not defeat the Vietnamese communists. Increasingly people throughout the world, including many in the USA itself, came to criticize US involvement in the war and the methods it was using. In 1969 the US began to gradually withdraw its troops, and in 1973 agreed to a cease-fire. Within two years North and South Vietnam were reunited and the whole of Indo-China had communist governments.

Why do you think the Americans failed? What clues does the following poem by Ho Chi Minh give you on how the Vietnamese felt?

> *Our rivers, our mountains, our men will always remain;*
> *The Yanks defeated, we will build our country ten times more beautiful.*[16]

This is what the US expert on foreign affairs and former Secretary of State, Henry Kissinger, had to say about the war:

> *It has created doubts about American judgment, about American credibility, about American power – not only at home, but throughout the world.*[17]

Do you think the Americans were wise to become involved in Vietnam?

The Middle East

Fear that Russia might gain control of some part of the Middle East first began in Britain two hundred years ago. In the 1850s Britain fought the Crimean War to stop Russian expansion. In the 1950s it became increasingly clear that the Middle East could not be kept out of the Cold War.

The anti-Soviet Baghdad Pact was set up in the area in 1955, and by then the first serious crisis was developing. President Nasser of Egypt refused to join the Baghdad Pact and arranged to buy Soviet weapons

A Soviet-made surface-to-air missile captured by the Israelis during the Six Day War, June 1967. The Israeli aircraft flew too low for the Egyptians to shoot them down.

through Czechoslovakia. The USA tried to win him over by offering financial help to build the Aswan Dam for hydro-electric power, and to help improve Egyptian agriculture. In the face of Nasser's connections with communist countries, however, the USA had second thoughts, and withdrew its offer. In retaliation Nasser nationalized the Suez Canal, which was owned by an international company controlled by the British and French.

Many people have thought, at the time and since, that Nasser was quite justified in wanting to control the canal which ran through his own country. The British Prime Minister, Sir Anthony Eden, however, was convinced that Nasser was a grave danger.

Gamal Abdel Nasser, president of Egypt 1956-70. Nasser obtained much economic and military aid from the USSR, and was thus seen as a threat to the West.

Eisenhower Doctrine was produced, reminiscent of the Truman Doctrine. It declared that the USA would support any Middle Eastern country which wanted its help against communism.

In 1958 US marines were landed in Lebanon to maintain the Eisenhower doctrine. These marines were serving in the US Sixth Fleet, a large force which patrols the Mediterranean. One of its aims was to support the USA's closest ally in the area – Israel. Israel has fought frequent wars with her Arab neighbours, and they have looked to the Soviet Union for help as Israel has looked to the USA. In 1973 the USA was so concerned that Russia would become involved against Israel in the Yom Kippur War that President Nixon even ordered nuclear forces to be ready for use.

In October 1956 he sent the following message to US President Eisenhower:

You can be sure that we are fully alive to the wider dangers of the Middle East situation. They can be summed up in one word – Russia . . . There can be no doubt in our minds that Nasser, whether he likes it or not, is now effectively in Russian hands.[18]

The British, French and Israelis invaded Egypt – a move which seemed to threaten world peace – and the Soviet Prime Minister Bulganin threatened to attack Britain. Eisenhower was appalled by the invasion and forced the three allies to withdraw.

The following year, in 1957, the

4

THE ARMS RACE
The nuclear threat

IN THE SUMMER OF 1945 the USA dropped the world's first two nuclear bombs on Japan. Forty years later, there were about 50,000 nuclear weapons in existence. Most of these belong to the USA and USSR. At the heart of the deadly rivalry of the two superpowers has been the arms race – an immensely costly competition to build more and 'better' weapons. Opinion on the effects of the nuclear arms race is divided. Some people think that this competition, with the horrendous danger of nuclear war, has made the Cold War more intense than it might otherwise have been. Others believe that it is only this threat that has kept world peace. The opinion of most Western governments has been that nuclear weapons exist not to be used but to deter the other side from war. This is called the theory of nuclear deterrence.

At first the Russians lagged behind in producing nuclear weapons, and for many years they were afraid that the USA might take advantage of its superiority. On the other hand, the West felt threatened by the larger 'conventional' (that is, non-nuclear) forces of the Warsaw Pact. NATO has therefore said it would be willing to be the first to use nuclear weapons if necessary to stop a Soviet attack. Is the term 'arms race' a good one? Can anyone win it?

Nuclear weapons can now be used for bombs, as warheads for rockets or artillery

A Soviet SS-1 battlefield nuclear missile. The SS-1 is capable of carrying either a nuclear warhead or a conventional high-explosive one. It has been used with the latter by Warsaw Pact armies, as well as by Egypt, Iraq, Libya and Syria.

shells. They can be launched from the ground, from aircraft or from submarines. Over the years different plans have been drawn up for possible situations in which they might be used. In the West, there have been five (the dates are approximate):

1 **Massive retaliation** (1950–62). The Americans could threaten to cause huge damage if the Russians attacked with conventional forces.

2 **Mutual assured destruction (MAD)** (1962–67). Once the Russians had caught up, both sides could threaten huge damage.

3 **Flexible response** (1967–82). Each side could select from its wide range of weapons depending on the circumstances.

A Lance battlefield nuclear weapon: it has a maximum range of 120 km, and can be deployed by helicopter, firing-platform, or self-propelled amphibious launcher. Many are stationed in West Germany.

4 **Counterforce** (1980 onwards). Missiles were developed which could hit a small target very accurately. It was now possible to hit the enemy's missile bases without, as before, destroying whole cities.

5 **Anti-missile defence** (1983 onwards). President Reagan ordered research into a scheme called the Strategic Defense Initiative (SDI) or 'Star Wars' as it has been called. The Russians are also undertaking similar research. The aim is to be able to destroy nuclear missiles before they reach their targets.

Summit Conferences

The Cold War has not been at a constant icy temperature since it started. On occasions the two sides have been able to show some understanding and friendship. This was so for a few years in the 1950s, a period sometimes known as 'the thaw'.

1953 was an important turning-point. In that year Eisenhower replaced Truman as US President, Stalin died, and the Korean War came to an end. The leaders of the USA, USSR, Britain and France decided to take the opportunity to meet in the hope of being able to reach an agreement on several problems and further relax the tension between the two sides. They met in 1955 in Geneva and in 1960 in Paris. These meetings were important for two reasons. Firstly, the leaders believed that only they could solve the current problems – the meetings had to be 'at the summit', only the topmost statesmen

A U-2 reconnaissance plane. These were used during the 1950s and 1960s to take aerial photographs from a great height. An incident involving a U-2 plane ruined the 1960 Paris Summit.

attended. Secondly, the summit meetings brought home the difficulty of the two sides reaching an agreement about nuclear weapons because the Russians tended to be so secretive.

The discussions were so cordial in 1955 that this new mood of friendship was referred to as 'the Geneva spirit'. The Russians proposed that all nuclear weapons should be scrapped. President Eisenhower, however, felt that he could not trust the Russians: how could the Americans be sure that they would not keep some? Instead Eisenhower presented his 'open skies for peace' plan. He proposed:

> to provide within our countries facilities for aerial photography to the other country . . . and by this step to convince the world that we are providing as between ourselves against the possibility of great surprise attack, thus lessening danger and relaxing tension.[19]

The Russians did not agree, but despite this a fortnight before the Paris summit meeting the USA sent a U-2 aircraft on a secret mission to photograph military bases in Russia. This was, of course, a form of spying. The aeroplane was shot down. In Paris Khrushchev demanded an apology from Eisenhower; he refused. Khrushchev was furious and broke up the conference.

When he reported the matter in Moscow, he said:

> They have been caught red-handed as the organizers of an incursion into the air space of the Soviet Union . . . But there are rules of international law, there are national frontiers and no one has the right to disregard those laws or to cross the frontiers of other countries.[20]

Do you think that these two summit meetings missed good opportunities to end the Cold War?

The four leaders at the Geneva summit conference in 1955. From left to right: Bulganin (USSR), Eisenhower (USA), Faure (France), Eden (Britain).

The Cuban missile crisis

U-2 spy aircraft, one of which ruined the 1960 Paris Summit, also played an important part in the incident which probably brought the world nearer to nuclear war than any other – the Cuban missile crisis.

In 1959 a group of Cubans led by Fidel Castro overthrew the unpopular Cuban government. The nationalization of US investments which followed led to a US economic boycott, and Castro turned to the Russians for trade and aid. The US Central Intelligence Agency wanted to overthrow Castro, but its attempt to do so by backing anti-Castro exiles failed and its defeat at the Bay of Pigs was disastrous. Why was the USA frightened of a communist government in Cuba?

At that time the Russians did not have nuclear missiles that could reach the USA, whereas the USA was able to reach Russia – for example from Turkey. To redress the balance Khrushchev arranged to install nuclear weapons in Cuba, and in October 1962 these were spotted and photographed by a U-2 spyplane. Russian ships transporting more were on their way.

The two Ks: President Kennedy and Chairman Khrushchev talking on friendly terms in Vienna in June 1961, sixteen months before the Cuban missile crisis.

President Kennedy had to decide what action to take. He ordered the navy to quarantine (blockade) Cuba, to stop any Soviet ships carrying missiles to Cuba, and demanded that those already installed be removed. All around the world people waited anxiously to see what would happen. After some hesitation, Khrushchev agreed to remove the missiles, on condition that the USA promised not to invade Cuba.

The crisis lasted thirteen days, and it raised very serious questions. First, how near had the world come to nuclear war? In a broadcast to the American people at the start of the crisis President Kennedy stated:

We will not prematurely or unnecessarily risk the costs of worldwide nuclear war in which even the fruits of victory would be ashes in our mouths – but neither will we shrink from that risk at any time it must be faced. [21]

Did Kennedy believe that the Russians would risk war? After the crisis, he said that

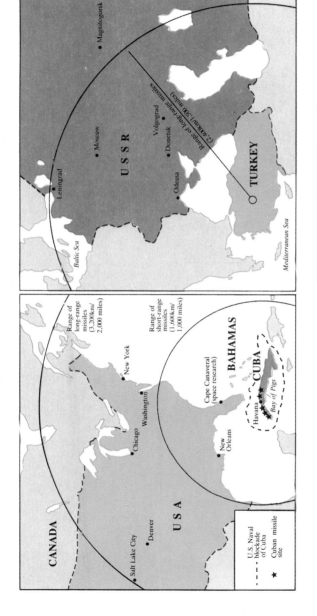

Relations between the USA and Cuba were very strained after Castro became the Cuban leader. He is seen here in 1960, in the middle of a three-hour speech attacking the USA.

Compare the potential threat of Soviet missiles in Cuba to the threat of US missiles already installed in Turkey.

he had estimated the odds as 'somewhere between one out of three and even's'.

The second question is, how skilfully did the two leaders handle the crisis? By ordering a blockade of Cuba instead of an attack, Kennedy won time for negotiation. Kennedy and Khrushchev exchanged messages and the Secretary-General of the United Nations acted as an intermediary. It was crucial that Khrushchev should be made to withdraw the missiles, but without 'losing too much face'. Kennedy achieved this by only replying to some of Khrushchev's messages and agreeing to their proposals. He repeated the outline of their agreement in a letter on 27 October:

1 You would agree to remove these weapons systems from Cuba under appropriate United Nations observation and supervision . . .

2 We, on our part, would agree . . . (a) to remove promptly the quarantine measures now in effect, and (b) to give assurances against an invasion of Cuba.[22]

Nuclear arms agreements

The Cuban missile crisis was handled by the exchange of telex messages – an extraordinarily slow method of conducting negotiations when every minute could count. Therefore in the following year a 'hot-line' was set up between the US and Soviet leaders. This is a teleprinter link for instant communication in the event of such a crisis. The scare also encouraged the two sides to take the search for agreements to control nuclear weapons more seriously.

The 1963 Partial Test Ban Treaty forbade nuclear testing in the atmosphere or under the water, but allowed underground tests. The USA, USSR and Britain signed and invited other countries to join them. Over ninety did so almost immediately, although several, including China and France, refused. Over the years three treaties have been signed to prohibit the placing of nuclear weapons in various areas: the Antarctic (1959), Latin America (1967) and Outer Space (1967). In 1968 the Non-Proliferation

Treaty was agreed on. Non-nuclear countries that signed it promised not to obtain nuclear weapons; countries with nuclear weapons promised not to supply them to non-nuclear states and also to negotiate seriously to reduce their number.

For many years the two superpowers did not seriously consider reducing the numbers of their nuclear weapons. They did, however, have talks to limit their increase. These were called Strategic Arms Limitation Talks (SALT) (1969–79) and led to two sets of treaties dealing with long-range weapons. SALT-I (1972) had two parts: one laid down figures for the various kinds of weapons (for instance bombers, missiles) each country was to have; the other part restricted the two countries to two ABM

A nuclear test. During the 1950s many people became concerned about the way the world was being poisoned by fall-out from the testing of nuclear weapons.

sites each. 'ABM' stands for Anti-Ballistic Missile, that is missiles to destroy missiles. In 1979 SALT-II was signed listing new limits for different long-range weapons. Why do you think nuclear disarmament has been so difficult? What does the graph below tell you about the effectiveness of the SALT treaties?

How and why do these extracts differ in the opinions they express on the SALT treaties?

They were really difficult and delicate matters we were working on; specialist delegations have spent almost three years, as of this August, on it. It is really a good end, a real milestone. (A. Gromyko, Soviet foreign minister on SALT-I)[23]

Neither SALT-I nor SALT-II committed either superpower to surrender any weapon that it really wished to keep. (Cambridge University Disarmament Seminar.)[24]

▲ The Soviet and US leaders, Brezhnev (on the right) and Nixon, signing the SALT-1 in Moscow in 1972.

◀ Graph showing the growth in number of strategic warheads in the arsenals of the USA and USSR from 1945-80.

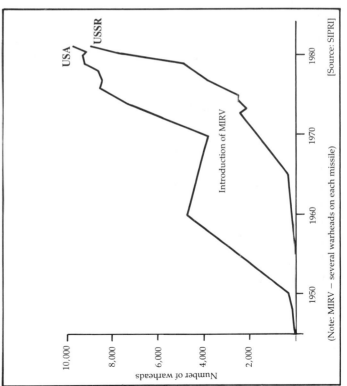

(Note: MIRV – several warheads on each missile)

35

5

THE EASTERN BLOC
Soviet political control

A rare photograph of political prisoners doing hard labour in a Stalinist prison camp. They are working in a quarry in the Dnieper region of the Ukraine.

ONE OF THE MAIN reasons for many in the West disliking the Soviet political system is that, at least until recently, it has allowed the Soviet people so little freedom. Many fear that the USSR may attempt to bring about communist governments in other countries, and look to the extension of Soviet control into Eastern Europe after the Second World War as proof of the USSR's desire to expand.

The Communist Party has extensive control of life behind the Iron Curtain. No other political parties and certainly no political opposition are allowed, and any communist politicians in the East European satellites who have tried to be at all independent have usually been removed by the Russian

government. The people of Eastern Europe have shown by several uprisings and strikes that they dislike the system – in East Germany in 1953, in Hungary in 1956, in Czechoslovakia in 1968, and in Poland in 1956, 1970, 1980–81 and 1988. Russian forces actually invaded Hungary and Czechoslovakia when new communist leaders there tried to rebel against Soviet control.

The communist system has depended very heavily on the political police, who have had the power to arrest, imprison, torture and even execute people who criticize wastes of the USSR. The other common method of repressing critics of the system has been to forcibly keep and 'treat' them in psychiatric hospitals.

Almost every government in the world has agreed to respect human rights – that is, to allow their people to live just and free lives. It is generally agreed that unrest and disturbances (such as those in Hungary, Czechoslovakia and Poland) are often the result when people are treated badly. Many Western politicians think that the Cold War will really end only when changes in Soviet political control occur. Partly, however, politicians use the issue of human rights as propaganda against Russia.

In 1975 the Russian leader Brezhnev signed an agreement in Helsinki in which he promised that his government would improve on the matter of human rights. This was like an admission that the West had a right to be concerned; but when US President Carter later tried to force some positive action, Brezhnev was angry and told him not to meddle in Russian affairs.

A photograph smuggled out the USSR of a psychiatric hospital. Political prisoners have been kept here.

the government. The worst examples of depriving people of their freedom have occurred in the Soviet Union itself. Especially while Stalin was leader, millions of Russians languished in labour camps strung out across the Arctic and Siberian

Riot police on duty in Warsaw, the capital of Poland, during a demonstration by students. This sort of scene has become commonplace in Poland.

37

The Hungarian Uprising

The most dramatic protest against Russian control occurred in Hungary in the autumn of 1956. On 23 October demonstrations against the Russians and the Hungarian political police started in the capital, Budapest, and soon spread to other parts of the country as Soviet tanks arrived. The old government resigned and Imre Nagy (pronounced *nodge*) formed a new government. The Russian troops left Hungary, but it soon became clear that Nagy wanted major changes and wanted Hungary to be neutral in the Cold War. The Russians could not allow this and on 4 November Soviet tanks were sent back to restore their own control. The Hungarians fought desperately and many fled to become refugees. Over 30,000 Hungarians died in the uprising, but the Russians overwhelmed the resistance. Nagy was arrested and was later executed.

These events were important in world affairs for four main reasons. Firstly, at the beginning of the uprising there was the problem of what Hungary's relations with Russia were to be. Nagy proclaimed Hungary neutral and demanded immediate negotiations for its withdrawal from the Warsaw Pact. This would, of course, have considerably weakened Russian control of Eastern Europe. If they allowed one member to leave, where would it end?

Secondly, the way the Russians crushed the uprising showed how ruthless they could be in achieving what they wanted. Many people in the West, including communists,

A Soviet truck being loaded with corpses: these people were victims during the uprising in Budapest in 1956.

In the 1950s the Hungarian secret police, the AVO, were bitterly hated. Many were murdered during the uprising in 1956 – one can be seen here dangling by the ankles from a tree.

were horrified by their action.

Thirdly, it is possible that the Hungarians were encouraged to stand up to the Russians because they believed that the USA might help them. The US Secretary of State, Dulles, had been constantly promising to 'liberate' the countries of Eastern Europe. The Russians in fact excused their action by accusing the West of stirring up the trouble. In his memoirs, Khrushchev wrote:

under whose sponsorship was the government of Imre Nagy created? In whose planes were waves of bourgeois agents and counter-revolutionary émigrés flown back into Hungary? The answer is, under the sponsorship and in the planes of the imperialistic forces of the world, especially the United States.[25]

The Hungarian uprising was complicated by the Suez crisis, which occurred at the same time and increased the tension between the USSR and the West. Eisenhower's speech-writer recalls how the President was worried by this complication:

For the obvious danger existed that Moscow might be irresistibly tempted toward aggressive action, on a massive scale, by both hope and fear – the hope that Egypt signified a deep division of the West, and the fear that Hungary threatened a kind of earthquake within the Soviet sphere.[26]

How do the relations between the superpowers at the time of the Hungarian uprising compare with those at the time of the 'Geneva spirit'?

Czechoslovakia and Poland

When Soviet tanks entered Prague in 1968 the people fought back, setting some of them on fire. This photograph was taken in August.

Twelve years after putting down the Hungarian uprising the Russian tanks were on the move again, this time to stop reform in Czechoslovakia. In April 1968, Alexander Dubček, who had recently been made Party Secretary, announced a programme of changes. This caused great excitement, especially in the capital, Prague. Dubček wanted 'socialism [communism] with a human face', and there were hopes that reforms would blossom in this 'Prague Spring'.

Brezhnev, the Soviet leader, declared his view of this in a statement known as the 'Brezhnev Doctrine':

We cannot agree to have hostile forces push your country away from Socialism and create a danger of Czechoslovakia being severed from the socialist community. This is something more than your own concern. It is the common concern of all the communist parties and states united by alliance, co-operation and friendship. The frontiers of the socialist world have moved to the Bohemian Forest. We shall never agree to these historic gains of Socialism . . . being put in danger. [27]

Does Brezhnev allow any hope for negotiating change or reforms? Six weeks later the tanks were sent in from Russia and other Warsaw Pact countries and Dubček was eventually removed from the government. What impact do you think the Brezhnev Doctrine had on the Cold War?

Poland has been different from many other satellites because a large proportion of the population are Roman Catholics and therefore oppose the atheist part of the communist doctrine. There have been several crises in Poland, the most important of which started in 1980. Protests about the dreadful state of the country's economy led to strikes, most notably by the workers in the shipyard at Gdansk. The leader of the workers was Lech Walesa (pronounced *lek vah-wensa*), and he formed a trade union, called Solidarity, which was completely independent of the Communist Party. Would the Russians invade? The situation was tense. Western governments prepared to respond. This is how a British journalist described the position:

> it was felt in all Western capitals that the Soviet leaders must not be allowed to think that East-West relationships would be patched up as rapidly as they were after the Warsaw Pact occupation of Czechoslovakia. They must be left in no doubt that an attack on Poland would lead to . . . a new Cold War.[28]

However, the Poles did not resort to violence even when the government made Solidarity illegal. There was no invasion. How might the events in Czechoslovakia have affected the Russians' reactions to unrest in Poland?

Lech Walesa (centre) became an extremely popular and influential leader when Polish workers protested against the government's mismanagement of the economy in 1980.

Human rights

Over the centuries the belief has gradually grown that human beings have certain inalienable rights. For example, no matter what your race, religion or political views, you should be able to expect just treatment at the hands of your government. Most people believe that you should not be arrested and imprisoned unless you have broken the law, you should be free to express your opinions, and you should not be tortured.

Many Russians, however, have been denied these human rights. After the death of Stalin, people tentatively began to criticize the government. Most of this criticism was in privately circulated writing (*samizdat*), but some of the dissidents were bolder and complained publicly and a number of them were punished by imprisonment. The great novelist Solzhenitsyn was forced to leave the Soviet Union.

After the Helsinki agreement groups were organized in a number of East European countries to press for reforms. The best

Andrei Sakharov has been called the father of the Soviet hydrogen bomb. More recently he has become famous for demanding more freedom in the USSR. He was awarded the Nobel Peace Prize in 1975.

known were Charter 77 in Czechoslovakia and the Helsinki Watch Groups in the USSR. The Soviet government, however, clamped down on this activity. The most famous campaigner, the physicist Sakharov, was sent to the town of Gorky and forbidden to leave. Another leader, Shcharansky, was accused of being an agent for the American CIA and was imprisoned for thirteen years for treason.

Jimmy Carter, US President from 1977 to 1981, tried to make the matter of human rights the most important part of his foreign policy, especially in relations with the USSR. In his memoirs he wrote:

the human rights issue . . . did create tension between us and prevented a more harmonious resolution of some of our other differences . . . The respect for human rights is one of the most significant advantages of a free and democratic nation in the peaceful struggle for influence, and we should use this good weapon as effectively as possible.[29]

Anatoly Shcharansky, the Soviet dissident, is seen here in February 1986 being released to the West across the Glienicke Bridge in Berlin, in exchange for captured communist spies. (Shcharansky is the one in the fur hat being led to the waiting car.) His release is an example of the attempts to improve relations between the superpowers in the late 1980s.

Should human rights matters be allowed to affect the relations between the USA and USSR?

In 1985 there was a change of government in Russia. Mikhail Gorbachev became party leader. He introduced a new policy of *glasnost*, or openness, allowing more opportunities to criticize the government. He also arranged for Sakharov to return to Moscow and for Shcharansky to be released. In 1986 he outlined four Fundamental Principles for international security. One of these was 'the humanitarian sphere' and included 'extension . . . of international co-operation in the implementation of the political, social, and personal rights of people.'[30]

6
CHANGING RELATIONS
Blowing hot and cold since 1972

DÉTENTE IS THE FRENCH word for relaxation, and is used to mean an easing of tension in international relations. This policy was pursued during much of the 1970s. Richard Nixon, who was US President from 1969–74, was a supporter of détente and had it put into effect by his foreign affairs expert, Dr Kissinger. The Soviet Union and China were also keen to improve relations with the USA.

Three important events mark the start of détente:

1 Visit by Nixon to Beijing to meet Mao Zedong, February 1972

2 Visit by Nixon to Moscow to sign SALT-1 treaty, May 1972

3 End of Vietnam War, January 1973

However, from 1979 to 1986 the blasts of a new Cold War chilled relations again. Many Americans felt that the USSR was taking advantage of détente, in particular by their sending help to left-wing movements in Africa. At the end of 1979 Soviet troops

In the civil war in Nicaragua the USA has supported the Contras in their fight against the Sandinista government. Here a supply of arms is being unpacked.

The meeting of Zhou Enlai, prime minister of China, and US President Nixon in China in 1972.

were sent into Afghanistan to fight in a civil war, but at the same time the USA was interfering in some of the small countries of Central America to weaken left-wing movements there. In 1981 Reagan was elected US President, promising to be 'tougher' with the Soviet Union and to spend much more money on weapons.

Hostility between the superpowers had now intensified again quite alarmingly. New nuclear weapons were being placed in Europe: SS-20s by the Russians and Pershing IIs and cruise missiles by the Americans. Then, in 1983, a most dramatic and tragic event occurred: Russian fighters shot down a South Korean airliner that was flying in Russian airspace. They thought it was spying for the Americans.

The USA now became increasingly worried by terrorism in the Middle East and suspected Russia of encouraging, or at least

gaining advantage from, these incidents. In 1979 a revolution took place in Iran and a number of Americans were taken hostage. The new Iranian government was connected with terrorism in the Lebanon. Then in 1980, what was to be a long drawn-out war broke out between Iraq and Iran. This affected the oil supplies from the Gulf that the West relied upon and again the USA feared Soviet interference.

When Gorbachev became Soviet leader in 1985 he quickly set about trying to ease international tension, declaring a policy of honesty and openness – *glasnost*. He was desperate to reduce the huge amount of money his country was spending on weapons. In November 1985 Gorbachev and Reagan held the first in a new series of summit meetings at Geneva; and then, in October 1986, they met at Reykjavik in Iceland. It was the start of a new phase of friendlier relations.

Why a New Cold War?

Détente was never meant to make the USA and the USSR close allies. Both sides recognized that competition, albeit of a more peaceful kind, would continue, and in any case such a long history of deep mistrust could not be wiped away quickly.

In both countries there were many influential people, particularly politicians, who opposed détente. Among these were older Russians who had lived through the crises of the early years of the Cold War, and

people in the USA who held strict Christian beliefs and hated atheist communism. In both East and West, arms manufacturers and senior officers in the armed services also objected to détente, for it affected their businesses and careers. In 1979–80 a number of events occurred to confirm their suspicions and the friendship of the 1970s quickly evaporated.

How far do you think the following statements explain the change in atmosphere?

Leonid Brezhnev, Soviet leader 1964-82. During the last years of his life he was ill and little progress could be made to improve relations between the USA and the USSR.

The first quotation is Brezhnev's response to US objections about Soviet intervention in Afghanistan.

Why did Washington fly into global hysterics? What is behind all the lies about a 'Russian war against the Afghan people', the 'Soviet threat to Pakistan and Iran', and so on? . . . The main motive is that the United States wants to set up a web of military bases in the Indian Ocean, in the countries of the Near East and Middle East, and in African countries. [31]

The second is from the first press conference Reagan held on becoming President.

So far détente's been a one-way street which the Soviet Union has used to pursue its own aims. I know of no leader of the Soviet Union, since the Revolution and including the present leadership, that has not more than once repeated . . . their determination that their goal must be the promotion of world revolution and a one-world socialist or communist state, . . . [and] they reserve the right to commit any crime, to lie, to cheat in order to obtain it. [32]

The Soviet Union placed new intermediate range missiles in Eastern Europe. The USA responded by placing its new missiles in Western Europe. In December 1979 Russian troops were sent to Afghanistan to help an unpopular communist government. The US Senate retaliated by refusing to ratify the SALT-II treaty. Events in Poland in the early 1980s made relations even more tense. Was one side any more to blame than the other in starting the Cold War again?

Row upon row of armoured vehicles and tanks can be seen in this Soviet camp in the centre of Afghanistan. During the 1980s there were many such camps. The Afghans' guerrilla tactics proved an effective resistance to such force, however.

Peace movements

French students protesting against the atomic bomb being tested in the Pacific Ocean.

The great English philosopher Bertrand Russell wrote in 1961: 'The history of disarmament conferences from Hiroshima to the present day is one of the most discouraging stories in human history.'[33] Three years before, he had helped to found the Campaign for Nuclear Disarmament (CND). Many people who felt strongly about the danger that these weapons posed to mankind demonstrated in protest marches. For a while the movement declined, but it revived with the onset of the New Cold War.

From about 1980 to 1986 three important groups organized protests against nuclear weapons in Britain: CND, Greenham Common, and END. A number of women set up a camp at Greenham Common in Berkshire, where US cruise missiles were stationed. The women objected to Britain being used as a launching-pad for such dangerous weapons. The European Nuclear Disarmament (END) movement was started to try to bring together protesters from both East and West Europe. In 1980 a leading member of END wrote:

The movement has taken off . . . In Britain this is true most of all. In every part of the country groups have been forming themselves, under many auspices and names – CND, World Disarmament, END, local councils of peace, and local campaigns against cruise missiles.[34]

Demonstrations took place in several European countries, particularly in Holland, West Germany and Romania. There were also strong peace movements in the USA, especially for a 'nuclear freeze', that is, for both sides to stop building any more nuclear weapons. Co-operation with the peace movement in the USSR was difficult because it has tended to be controlled by the government.

Many people, however, believe that the

A mass anti-nuclear rally in London, with thousands of CND supporters. The 1980s saw many such demonstrations in Britain as a reaction to large increases in weaponry.

protesters are badly mistaken. There are two main opposition arguments. First, that nuclear weapons are not meant to be used, but to deter; and indeed there has been no war in Europe since 1945, or between the superpowers. The second argument is against unilateral disarmament, by which countries in the West would give up nuclear weapons without an agreement for equal disarmament by the Soviet Union. This is what the British Conservative Party had to say about unilateral disarmament:

That policy . . . would expose us to nuclear blackmail from the vast Soviet armoury, to which we would have no reply. It would inflict damage, perhaps fatal damage, on the Atlantic Alliance on which we in Western Europe depend for our security . . . It would, in short, be the biggest victory for the Soviet Union in 40 years. [35]

Arms negotiations

In 1982 new talks started in Geneva, aimed at an agreement to *reduce* the numbers of US and Soviet nuclear weapons. There were, however, very difficult obstacles to overcome.

1 Were the two governments really serious in wanting nuclear disarmament?

2 Was it possible to deal with nuclear weapons separately from conventional weapons? How could they take into account the larger numbers of Warsaw Pact troops in Europe compared with NATO (which talks in Vienna have been trying to tackle)? And what about chemical weapons (poison gases)?

3 How would one count the Russian nuclear weapons in Asia, defending the long frontier with China?

4 How can one compare completely different kinds of nuclear weapons, for example long-range and short-range? Do you count the numbers of 'launchers' (bombers and missiles) or the numbers of warheads and bombs?

A US Pershing-II. This is one of the missiles which the superpowers agreed to destroy in the 1987 INF treaty.

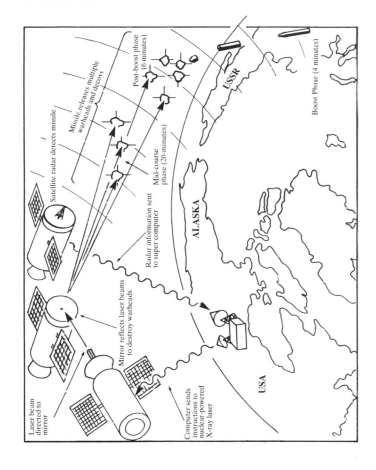

The basic idea of the Strategic Defense Initiative is that space-based laser systems will destroy missiles before they reach their target.

Laser beam directed to mirror

Satellite radar detects missile

Missile releases multiple warheads and decoys

Post-boost phase (6 minutes)

Mirror reflects laser beams to destroy warheads

Mid-course phase (20 minutes)

Radar information sent to super computer

Computer sends instructions to nuclear-powered X-ray laser

USA

ALASKA

USSR

Boost Phase (4 minutes)

5 If an agreement is reached to destroy stocks of nuclear weapons, how can each side be sure that the other is not cheating?

These problems were further complicated by Reagan's plan for a Strategic Defense Initiative (SDI, commonly known as 'Star Wars'). In 1983 he made a speech in which he said:

I call upon the scientific community who gave us nuclear weapons to turn their great talents to the cause of mankind and world peace: to give us the means of rendering these nuclear weapons impotent and obsolete.[36]

The purpose of SDI is to develop a system to destroy enemy missiles in space, before they reach their target. The new plan worried the Russians and upset the calculations of the experts trying to reduce numbers of weapons in a balanced way. Was Reagan right to suggest SDI would improve world peace?

When Reagan and Gorbachev met at Reykjavik in 1986 they very nearly reached an agreement on enormous reductions in nuclear weapons. However, Gorbachev would not commit himself unless Reagan gave up 'Star Wars'. Reagan refused. Nevertheless, in 1987 the two leaders signed a treaty in Washington, agreeing to destroy land-based INF weapons (Intermediate Nuclear Force – weapons with a range of 500–5,000 kilometres). The treaty included details of how each side would inspect the way the other was dismantling its missiles. The next stage was to be a START (Strategic Arms Reduction Talks) treaty. These talks, which had been interrupted after their beginning in 1982, were now resumed.

Meanwhile, further ideas were produced, including the possibility of reducing conventional (that is, non-nuclear) forces in Europe. By 1988 the relations between East and West were still delicate, but there was now more optimism than ever that the Cold War could be replaced by an easier and less suspicious relationship between the two superpowers.

Leading figures

Bevin, Ernest (1881–1951) British Foreign Secretary 1945–51

Bevin gained a reputation as a very skilful trade union organizer and negotiator. He entered politics in 1940 when Churchill made him Minister of Labour. In 1945 Attlee made him Foreign Secretary in his Labour government. He became famous for the blunt, working-class manner in which he conducted affairs. He is important for his part in approving the Marshall Plan and in strengthening Western defence arrangements. In particular he persuaded the Americans of the necessity for NATO.

Brezhnev, Leonid Ilyich (1906–82) Soviet politician

Brezhnev was trained as an engineer but worked as a political commissar with the army during the Second World War. His career in the Communist Party was helped by his friendship with Khrushchev. He was President of the Soviet Union from 1960–64 and 1977–82. He was head of the government as First Secretary of the Party from 1964 until his death. Brezhnev allowed few changes to occur inside Russia. He had dissidents arrested and prevented Russian Jews from emigrating to Israel. He also failed to prevent a great deal of corruption developing within the Party. In foreign affairs he stopped the reforms in Czechoslovakia in 1968 and forbade any such changes in Eastern Europe in his Brezhnev Doctrine. He nevertheless met several US Presidents and signed both SALT treaties. Brezhnev was ill for several years before his death, by which time it was clear that the Soviet Union needed more vigorous leadership.

Eisenhower, Dwight D. (1890–1969) US general and politician

Eisenhower was a professional soldier and served with distinction in the Second World War, during which he commanded the Allied forces in the invasion of France in 1944. When NATO was created he became SACEUR (Supreme Allied Commander in Europe). As a general he was particularly skilful in persuading his commanders to work together. His nickname was 'Ike' and his popularity was shown by the slogan 'I like Ike'. He was President from 1953–61, having won the election by a huge majority. His easy-going manner led some people to accuse him of laziness, but it helped to strengthen friendly relations between the USA and Britain and to produce the cordial atmosphere at the 1955 Geneva Summit Conference. Eisenhower was genuinely concerned that the arms race was getting out of hand.

Gorbachev, Mikhail S. (1931–) Soviet politician

After the death of Brezhnev the Soviet Union had two aged 'stop-gap' leaders. Then, in 1985 Gorbachev, a younger man, became General Secretary. He had studied law at Moscow University and then worked for the Communist Party. He soon made a great impact, both in the USSR and in the world. He immediately set out to make himself known, cleverly using television and newspapers to explain his policies. His two key words have been *glasnost* and *perestroika*, meaning openness and restructuring. Gorbachev has encouraged discussion about problems and set about reforming the Soviet administration and economy. He wishes to use more of Russia's wealth for peaceful rather than military purposes, and he believes nuclear weapons are extremely dangerous. He has made great attempts to obtain agreements on disarmament with the USA. As well as being leader of the Communist Party, in 1988 he became President of the USSR.

The Soviet leader Gorbachev and US President Reagan in conversation during their summit meeting in Geneva in 1985.

Ho Chi Minh (1890–1969) Vietnamese communist revolutionary leader

Ho Chi Minh had an extremely varied career before devoting himself to freeing Indo-China from French control. He was a founder member of the French Communist Party and later founded the Vietminh organization in Indo-China. During the Second World War he fought against the Japanese, who occupied Indo-China. At the end of the war the French tried to take back control; Ho led the resistance against them and became President of North Vietnam when the French were defeated. When the Vietcong fought the South Vietnam government and the Americans, Ho sent supplies to help. After the USA bombed North Vietnam, the people rallied round Ho who was very popular indeed. When Vietnam was reunited, Saigon was renamed Ho Chi Minh City in his honour.

Kennedy, John F. (1917–63) US politician

After war service Kennedy was a member of Congress, 1946-60. When he won the Presidential election in 1960 he became the youngest President in US history and the only Roman Catholic to hold the office. He was very committed to social reform at home (his 'new frontier' policy) and in Latin America (for which he founded a 'Peace Corps'). In the Cold War he was a sturdy rival to Khrushchev, and they were popularly known as 'the two Ks'. He refused to bow to Soviet pressure to withdraw from Berlin; and the two leaders confronted each other most dramatically in the Cuban missile crisis. While on a visit to Dallas, Texas he was assassinated.

Khrushchev, Nikita S. (1894–1971) Soviet politician

After fighting in the Russian civil war and working as a miner, Khrushchev worked for the Communist Party. He was Prime Minister of the Ukraine (part of the USSR) from 1944–47. After the death of Stalin he was the most important Soviet leader. He was First Secretary of the Party 1953–64, and Prime Minister 1958–64. In 1956 he made a dramatic speech, bitterly criticizing Stalin. He also reduced the power of the secret police. In the Cold War Khrushchev said that the relations between the two sides should be 'peaceful co-existence'. He was involved in several important crises, including the quarrel with China and the Cuban missile incident. Khrushchev had a colourful personality and a short temper. He made enemies in the Soviet Union and was forced to resign in 1964.

Mao Zedong (1893–1976) Chinese communist leader

Although Mao helped to found the Chinese Communist Party, he changed its ideas by emphasizing the importance of the peasantry and guerrilla warfare rather than factory workers and urban uprisings for bringing about revolution. When the communists were surrounded by the Chinese government army he led the incredible Long March (1934–35) to set up a new base. The march of 9,650 kilometres took one year. There followed a lengthy civil war, which the communists won in 1949. Mao was Chairman of the People's Republic of China 1949–59, and of the Party 1949–76. Mao tried to keep up the pace of revolutionary change and imprisoned or executed many of his opponents. Some of his policies brought chaos and famine to China. After his quarrel with the Soviet Union in the 1960s he was willing to become friendlier with the USA – a complete reversal of China's previous policy. He met President Nixon in 1972.

Nixon, Richard M. (1913–) US politician

Nixon first became famous as a lawyer in the late 1940s prosecuting suspected spies. He was Eisenhower's Vice-President from 1953–61, and he was President himself from 1969–74, during which time he brought the Vietnam War to an end, established friendly relations with China and signed the SALT-I treaty. He was forced to resign after the 'Watergate' scandal, in which it was revealed that he had used his presidential status to carry out a secret raid on the opposing Democratic Party's headquarters. This seemed to confirm his reputation as 'tricky Dick'.

Reagan, Ronald W. (1911–) US politician

Before entering politics Reagan made a number of films in Hollywood. He was Governor of California from 1967–74, and President from 1981–89 (the oldest person ever to hold the office). Originally a staunch liberal, he became a hard-line conservative in the 1950s. Until the mid-1980s he expressed intense dislike of the Soviet Union and emphasized his own deeply-held belief in the salvation of good Christians. Partly because of these beliefs and partly because of his skilful use of television appearances, he was extremely popular with the American people. However, those who worked for him were worried by his apparent laziness and lack of understanding of political affairs. Nevertheless, he came to recognize the importance of friendlier relations with the Soviet Union and signed the INF treaty in 1987.

Stalin, Joseph V. (1879–1953) Soviet politician

Stalin was born in a village in the Caucasus region. He made an important contribution to the Russian civil war in defending a city

Harry S. Truman, US president 1945-53.

which was thereafter renamed Stalingrad. After the death of Lenin he out-manoeuvred Trotsky to the leadership. He then set about making the Soviet Union a powerful country. He was utterly ruthless in dealing with peasants who wanted to keep their land and with anyone who opposed him. Many millions died or suffered in labour camps. He forced people almost to worship him in the 'cult of personality'. During the Second World War he led his country in the intensely bitter conflict with Germany and as a result became popular in the West as 'Uncle Joe'. However, after the war his suspicious nature made him imprison many of his own people and rendered the Cold War more intense than perhaps it might otherwise have been.

Truman, Harry S. (1884–1972) US politician

In his early public life Truman served as a judge and a senator. He became Roosevelt's Vice-President in 1945 only eleven weeks before the President's death on which he suddenly had to take over as President. He held the office until 1953 and had to cope with the end of the Second World War and the start of the Cold War. It was Truman who decided to drop the atomic bombs on Japan, and who issued the Truman Doctrine in 1947 which worsened the tension with the USSR. He was also President during most of the Korean War. Some historians believe the Cold War would not have been quite so intense if Roosevelt had not died when he did.

Important dates

Date	Events
1917	*October/November* Bolshevik Revolution
1918–20	Civil War in Russia
1939–40	Occupation of land lost in 1918 in Eastern Europe by USSR
1939–45	Second World War
1945	*February* Yalta Conference
	Partition of Germany and Korea
1945–48	Establishment of communist governments in Eastern Europe
1945–53	Harry S. Truman, US President
1946	*March* Churchill's 'Iron Curtain' speech
1947	*March* Truman Doctrine announced
	June Marshall Plan announced
	October Establishment of the Cominform
1948–49	Berlin blockade
1949	*April* Creation of NATO
	October Creation of the People's Republic of China (PRC)
1949–76	Mao Zedong, Chairman of the Chinese Communist Party
1950–53	Korean War
1953	*March* Death of Stalin
1953–59	John Foster Dulles, US Secretary of State
1953–61	Dwight D. Eisenhower, US President
1953–64	N. S. Khrushchev, Soviet Party Secretary
1954	Partition of Vietnam
1955	*May* Creation of the Warsaw Pact
	July Geneva Summit Conference
	Creation of the Baghdad Pact
1956	*October–November* Suez crisis
	October–November Hungarian uprising
1957	*January* Eisenhower Doctrine announced
1958	*February* Start of Campaign for Nuclear Disarmament (CND)
1959	Castro in control of Cuba
1960	*May* Paris Summit Conference and U-2 spy plane incident
	Intensification of split between USSR and China
1961	*August* Berlin Wall started
1961–63	John F. Kennedy, US President
1962	*October* Cuban missile crisis
1963	*June* Establishment of 'hot-line'
	July Partial Test-Ban Treaty
1964–73	Main period of US involvement in Vietnam War
1964–82	L. I. Brezhnev, Soviet Party Leader
1968	'Prague Spring' and Brezhnev Doctrine
1969–74	Richard M. Nixon, US President
1972	*February* Visit of Nixon to Beijing
	May SALT-I Treaty
1973	*October* Yom Kippur War

1973–77	Dr Henry Kissinger, US Secretary of State
1975	European Security Conference held in Helsinki
1977–81	Jimmy Carter, US President
1979	*January* Start of revolution in Iran
	June SALT-II Treaty
	December Soviet intervention in Afghanistan
1980	*August* Founding of Polish trade union, Solidarity
	September Start of the Iran-Iraq War
1981–89	Ronald Reagan, US President
1982	*July* Start of Geneva nuclear disarmament talks
1983	*March* Reagan's 'Star Wars' speech
	August Shooting down of Korean airliner
1985	*March* Mikhail Gorbachev elected General Secretary of Soviet Communist Party
1986	*October* Reykjavik Summit meeting
1987	*December* INF Treaty
1988	Start of Soviet troop withdrawals from Afghanistan
	End of Iran-Iraq war

Glossary

Arsenal
Stock of weapons.

Atheist
Belief that there is no God.

Bloc
A group of countries combined by a common interest or aim.

Bolshevik
Russian Communist Party which gained control of the government in the October revolution of 1917.

Capitalism
An economic theory that believes in the virtue of free enterprise, and the right to individual property and wealth.

CIA
US Central Intelligence Agency, created in 1947 to conduct intelligence and espionage activities. The CIA secretly supports countries friendly to the USA and undermines those considered hostile.

Communism
A political and economic theory based on the ideas of Karl Marx, who believed in abolition of private property and the creation of a classless society.

Congress
The House of Representatives and the Senate – the two US law-making assemblies.

Containment
A principle of US foreign policy that seeks to prevent the expansion of communist power.

Counter-revolutionary
Working against the revolution, that is against the interests of the Soviet Union which supports the idea of communist revolutions.

Cruise
US medium-range nuclear missile which can be launched from air, sea or land. It can fly very low and is therefore hard to detect.

Demobilize
To disband an army – for example, at the end of a war when not so many forces are needed.

Détente
Easing of tension between nations.

Deterence
The theory that the fear of nuclear destruction will stop a country from behaving aggressively.

Dissident
Someone who disagrees with their government, especially a political opponent in the USSR.

Emigrés
People who have fled from their own country for political reasons.

Glasnost
Russian for openness. The term is used for Gorbachev's policy of allowing more openness, both in internal and international affairs.

Guerrilla
A form of warfare conducted by small mobile bands of troops against a regular army.

Hostage
A person held prisoner by an organization, whose life or freedom might then be bargained with, usually in the hope of achieving a political aim or gaining money.

Human rights
Certain rights all people should be allowed, for example, liberty, justice, freedom from torture and imprisonment without trial.

Ideology
A body of ideas which reflects the beliefs and interests of a nation or political system.

Imperialism
Policy of extending a state's rule over other territories, often through aggression.

Liberate
Set free from enemy occupation.

NATO
North Atlantic Treaty Organization – a military alliance of Western nations.

Nationalize
To put an industry under state control or ownership.

Perestroika
Russian for restructuring. The term is used for Gorbachev's policy of restructuring Soviet administration.

Propaganda
Carefully selected information, usually given out through broadcasting and newspapers, designed to direct people's views.

Purge
Elimination of political rivals by imprisonment and/or execution.

Ratification
Gaining the formal approval (for example by the Senate in the USA, and the Supreme Soviet in the USSR) necessary to make a treaty come into effect.

Repression
Political control by force; for example, by censorship and imprisonment of opponents.

Satellite
A nation that is highly dependent on another for economic support and political direction. For example, those countries of Eastern Europe controlled by the USSR: East Germany, Poland, Czechoslovakia, Hungary, Romania and Bulgaria.

Senate
The upper chamber of the US law-making assembly.

Socialism
An economic and political theory that believes that the state should own all important means of production and distribution of wealth, and stresses the social principle of equality – in contrast to capitalism.

Star Wars
Popular name for the US Strategic Defense Initiative (SDI).

Strategic weapons
Designed to attack a target from a long distance away, e.g. missiles with a range of more than 3,000 kilometres.

Summit meeting
A meeting of the major world leaders – often only from the USA and USSR – to discuss issues of highest importance.

Superpowers
States that are very much stronger than most others. Usually refers to the USA and USSR.

Terrorism
Use of violence or intimidation (e.g. bombing, kidnapping) to force a government to agree to demands.

Totalitarian
A dictatorial state in which one party controls all aspects of life.

Unification
To make a number of regions or states into one, such as where a country has been divided and is restored to being one nation.

United Nations
International organization established in 1945 to promote peace and international co-operation.

Warsaw Pact
A military alliance of countries in the Eastern bloc – the USSR and its satellite states.

Witch-hunt
Hunting out opponents (e.g. communists), as witches were once hunted, claiming them to be a threat to the country's security.

Further reading

Elementary

Barker, E., *The Cold War*, Wayland, 1972.
Barnes, R., *Ideology and the Cold War*, Tressell, 1984.
Cox, J., *Overkill*, Penguin, 1981.
Rees, D., *The Age of Containment*, Macmillan, 1967.
Simkin, J., *American Foreign Policy*, Spartacus, 1986.

Advanced

Chomsky, N., Steele, J., Gittings, J., *Superpowers in Collision*, Penguin, 1984.
Halliday, F., *The Making of the Second Cold War*, Verso, 1983.
Horowitz, D., *From Yalta to Vietnam*, Penguin, 1967.
Prins, G. (ed.) *Defended to Death*, Penguin, 1983.
Wilson, A., *The Disarmer's Handbook*, Penguin, 1983.
Yergin, D., *Shattered Peace*, Penguin, 1977.

Sources

Hanak, H., *Soviet Foreign Policy since the Death of Stalin*, Routledge & Kegan Paul, 1972.
McCauley, M., *The Origins of the Cold War*, Longman, 1983.

Picture acknowledgements

The author and publishers would like to thank the following for allowing their illustrations to be used in this book: Camera Press 5, 12, 20, 22, 26, 28, 29, 30, 34, 37 (bottom), 38, 39, 40, 41, 42, 44, 47, 48, 49, 50; Popperfoto 4, 6, 7 (top & bottom), 9 (top, centre, bottom), 10, 11, 13, 14, 16, 17 (bottom), 18, 19, 21, 23, 25, 27, 31, 32, 33, 35, 36, 37 (top), 45; Rex Features Ltd. cover; Frank Spooner 17 (top), 43; Topham 46, 53; Wayland Picture Library 55. The artwork was supplied by Thames Cartographic Services Ltd.

Notes on sources

1 N. S. Khrushchev, *Khrushchev Remembers*, vol. 2, London, 1974.
2 Speech, 8 March 1983.
3 *Foreign Affairs*, vol. 25, July 1947.
4 J. Stalin, *Problems of Leninism*, Moscow, 1945.
5 Speech, 5 March 1946.
6 Speech, 12 March 1947.
7 Milovan Djilas, *Conversations with Stalin*, Harmondsworth, 1963.
8 Harry S. Truman, *Years of Trial and Hope*, New York, 1958.
9 Report to the Nation, 25 July 1961.
10 John Vaizey, *The Squandered Peace*, London, 1983.
11 Daniel Yergin, *Shattered Peace*, Harmondsworth, 1980.
12 T. E. Vadney, *The World Since 1945*, Harmondsworth, 1987.
13 Article 5.
11 Research Center for Peace and Unification, *Korea's Quest for Peaceful Unification*, Seoul, 1978.
15 Alfred Crofts, 'Our Falling Ramparts – The Case of Korea', *The Nation*, 25 June 1960.
16 Quoted in Michael Maclear, *Vietnam: The Ten Thousand Day War*, London, 1981.
17 Quoted in Stanley Karnow, *Vietnam: A History*.
18 Anthony Eden, *Full Circle*, London, 1960.
19 Quoted in Robert J. Donovan, *Eisenhower: The Inside Story*, New York, 1956.
20 Speech to the Supreme Soviet, 7 May 1960.

21 Radio and Television Report to the American People, 22 October 1962.
22 Letter, President Kennedy to Chairman Khrushchev, 27 October 1962.
23 Quoted in Henry Kissinger, *The White House Years*, London, 1979.
24 Gwyn Prins (ed.), *Defended to Death*, Harmondsworth, 1983.
25 N. S. Khrushchev, *Khrushchev Remembers*, vol. 1, London, 1971.
26 E. J. Hughes, *The Ordeal of Power*, London, 1963.
27 Letter from L. I. Brezhnev to A. Dubček, 15 July 1968.
28 Neal Ascherson, *The Polish August*, Harmondsworth, 1981.
29 Jimmy Carter, *Keeping Faith*, London, 1982.
30 Mikhail Gorbachev, *Political Report of the CPSU Central Committee to the 27th Party Congress*, Moscow, 1986.
31 Speech in Moscow, 22 February 1980.
32 Press conference statement, 30 January 1981.
33 Bertrand Russell, *Has Mankind a Future?*, Harmondsworth, 1961.
34 E. P. Thompson & Dan Smith, *Protest and Survive*, Harmondsworth, 1980.
35 Conservative Central Office, *Election Manifesto: The Next Moves Forward*, London, 1987.
36 Quoted in E. P. Thompson (ed.), *Star Wars*, Harmondsworth, 1985.

Index

Figures in **bold** refer to illustrations.